FISH FARMS

FUNKY FARMS

Lynn M. Stone

The Rourke Corporation, Inc.
Vero Beach, Florida 32964

PHOTO CREDITS:
All photos © Lynn M. Stone, except page 10: © Jerry Hennen;
page 8: © Breck Kent

ACKNOWLEDGMENT:
The author thanks Scott Barnes and Rushing Water Fisheries of Palmyra, Wisconsin, for their cooperation and support in the preparation of this book.

EDITORIAL SERVICES:
Susan Albury

CREATIVE SERVICES:
East Coast Studios, Merritt Island, Florida

Library of Congress Cataloging-in-Publication Data

Stone, Lynn M.
    Fish farms / by Lynn M. Stone
        p. cm. — (Funky farms)
    Summary: Describes the physical characteristics and habits of some species of fish and how they are raised on farms across the United States.
    ISBN 0-86593-543-2
    1. Fish—culture Juvenile literature.   [1. Fish—culture.] I. Title.
II. Series: Stone, Lynn M. Funky farms.
SH151.S76 1999
639.3—dc21   99-25913
                                                                  CIP

Printed in the USA

TABLE OF CONTENTS

FISH

Fish are an important food in many nations, including the United States and Canada. They are also important for the sport they offer fishermen.

Fish live in seas, streams, ponds, and lakes. Most fish have slick, scaly skins and fins.

Like whales, which also live in the water, fish have backbones. But whales must rise to the water's surface to breathe air. Fish breathe underwater using their gills, which allows them to get oxygen from water.

Whales, like humans, are mammals. Fish belong to their own separate group of animals.

Fish like this wild sockeye salmon are a rich source of sport and food.

FISH FARMS

Because fish are in great demand, fish farms raise them. If people ate only wild fish, some kinds would become **extinct** (ik STINKT), or disappear.

Fish farmers practice a type of **aquaculture** (AW kwah kul chur). Aquaculture is the raising, or farming, of **aquatic** (aw KWAH tik) animals or plants. Animals and plants that live in the water are aquatic.

6

Salmon are raised on fish farms and in hatcheries. They are a favorite food and sport fish. This silver salmon is a wild fish, taken from Alaska's Kenai River.

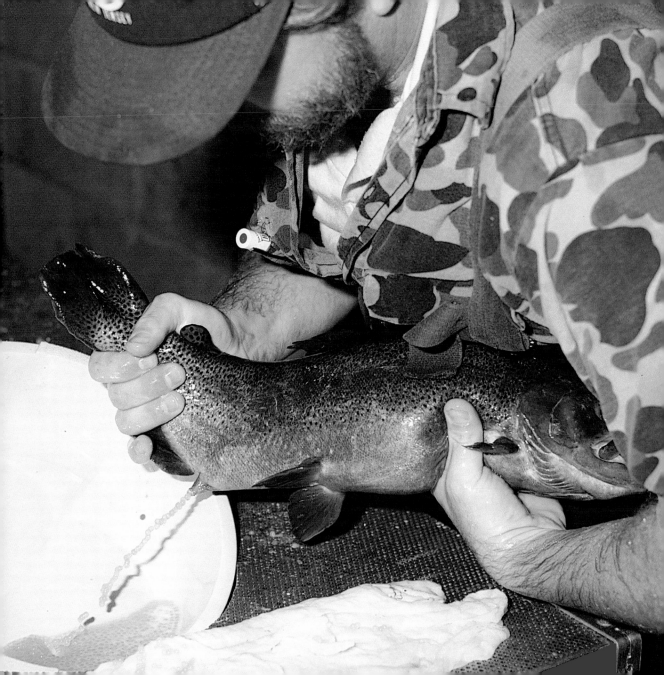

Fish aren't the only aquatic animals being farmed. Some of the others are turtles, shrimp, lobster, oysters, clams, and **mussels** (MUS sulz).

Fish farmers raise only a few of the thousands of **species** (SPEE sheez), or kinds of fish. They raise fish that can be easily sold for food or for sport.

Farms that raise sport fish are often called **hatcheries** (HAT chur eez). A hatchery can also be any farm that raises fish from eggs.

The release of hatchery-raised sport fish into the wild is called **stocking** (STAW king). Hatchery fish help rebuild the number of wild fish.

Hatcheries produce fish eggs. This stream of eggs is being stripped, or squeezed, from an adult female rainbow trout.

HOW FISH FARMS BEGAN

Some fish can be raised quite easily. Carp, for example, which are related to goldfish, take little care.

About 4,000 years ago, the ancient Chinese discovered that they could raise certain kinds of fish very simply. With the first fish farms, the Chinese made life easier. No longer did they have to go fishing for a fish dinner.

Today China is the world's largest **producer** (pruh DOO sur) of farm-raised freshwater fish. But fish farming has spread throughout the world, wherever people enjoy fish and fishing.

Fresh from their eggs, tiny fish live for five or six days off the puffy food sacs you can see below their heads.

A fish farmer feeds scoops of pellets to trout in a spring-fed Wisconsin pond. The net above the pond protects fish from...

...fish eating visitors, like ospreys (fish hawks) and this heron.
The heron found its fish dinner elsewhere.

FARM FISH

Most fish farms in the United States raise salmon, trout, or freshwater catfish. Trout and salmon are raised for both food and sport. Catfish are raised largely for food.

In much smaller numbers, American fish farms also raise striped bass, African tilapia (tuh LAH pee uh), and a few other species for food. Farms raise several kinds of sport fish and aquarium fish.

Some of the food species raised overseas include halibut, turbot, and carp.

A fish farmworker holds a market-sized rainbow trout. Trout are one of the most popular fish from freshwater fish farming.

RAISING FISH

Fish are raised in tanks, ponds, and in ocean cages, depending upon the kind of fish. Farm fish live mostly on food pellets (PEL lutz) provided by the farmers. In some natural ponds and pens at sea the fish also eat wild foods.

One of the popular farm-raised fish in American markets and restaurants is trout. Many species of trout live in North America. Most trout farmers raise the colorful, fast-growing rainbow.

16

Rainbow trout are hauled from fish ponds to be graded, or put into groups. Farmers like to keep fish of the same size together.

A farmer may buy trout eggs or baby trout to start a fish crop. A farmer who buys eggs keeps them in trays filled with water. The water temperature must stay cool, about 48 degrees Fahrenheit (9 degrees Celsius).

The trout hatch after five or six days. They spend the next six or seven months in indoor tanks. The farmer first feeds them powdery fish food. Later, the farmer feeds the trout food pellets.

At about seven months of age, the trout are moved into outdoor ponds. The water temperature must not become too hot or too cold.

The trout live outdoors for almost a year. By then, they weigh just over one pound (.5 kilogram). At that size, the farmer nets the trout from the ponds. They are ready for market.

A farmer tosses food pellets to trout in an outdoor tank. When these trout grow larger, they will be placed in ponds.

Atlantic salmon are raised in freshwater for about 18 months for the food market. Then they are moved to sea pens. After 18 to 24 months at sea, they are taken to market at about 8 pounds (3.6 kilograms).

Farm fish are killed, **gutted** (GUHT id), and readied for market very quickly. For example, a trout may be swimming in a Wisconsin fish farm pond on a Monday morning. By Monday evening it's on a plate in a Chicago restaurant 100 miles (160 kilometers) away.

Sharp knives and quick, sure hands turn rainbow trout into boneless portions of meat called fillets.

FISH FARMS IN THE FUTURE

Fish farms have a bright future. Rivers, lakes, and oceans cannot produce enough wild fish to satisfy the demand. As long as people have a taste for fish, fish farming will grow.

Meanwhile, scientists are working hard to learn more about how to improve water quality and fish foods. Farmers want fish to gain weight quickly.

Other researchers are working to enlarge the roles of computers and electricity at fish farms.

GLOSSARY

aquaculture (AW kwah kul chur) — the raising, or farming, of aquatic animals and plants

aquatic (aw KWAH tik) — refers to those plants and animals that live in water

extinct (ik STINKT) — referring to a kind of plant or animal completely gone from the earth, such as dinosaurs

gutted (GUHT id) — to have the insides, or gut removed from an animal; to be cleaned after slaughter

hatchery (HAT chur ee) — a place that produces fish eggs and, often, very young fish; a place where fish hatch from eggs

mussel (MUS sul) — a hard-shelled, boneless animal closely related to clams and oysters; a type of mollusk found largely in salt water

pellet (PEL lut) — a small, rounded piece of food, often made up of tiny bits of many foods

producer (pruh DOO sur) — anyone or anything that raises, or produces, something

species (SPEE sheez) — within a group of closely related animals, one certain kind, such as the rainbow trout

stocking (STAW king) — the act or process of putting hatchery fish into nature, such as a river or pond

INDEX

FURTHER READING

Find out more about fish with these helpful books and information sites:
Cater, Kyle. *What Makes a Fish?* Rourke, 1997.
Parker, Steve. *Fish* Knopf. 1990

AquaNIC online at ag.ansc.purdue.edu/aquanic
Sea Grant Institute 1800 University Avenue, Madison, Wisconsin 53705-4094
    on line at www.seagrant.wisc.edu/Advisory/Aquaculture/index.html
Wisconsin Aquaculture Association
    on line at www.wisconsinaquaculture.com